THE WEIGHT OF IRISES

For Norman —
With much love &
thanks. Missing
you!

B.

THE WEIGHT OF IRISES

NICOLETTE STASKO

Black Pepper
Melbourne, Australia

First published by *Black Pepper*
403 St George's Road, North Fitzroy, Victoria 3068

National Library of Australia
Cataloguing-in-Publication data:

     Stasko, Nicolette
     The weight of irises
     ISBN 1 876044 39 X

     I.   Title

A821.3

Cover image: Julian Merrow-Smith
Cover design: Gail Hannah

 This project has been assisted by the
Commonwealth Government through the
Australia Council, its art funding and
advisory body.

Acknowledgments

Some of these poems have previously appeared in *Antipodes* (USA), *HEAT, Island, Overland, Southerly, SALT, Salt-lick Quarterly, Thylazine, Ulitarra, Stand* (Britain) and been anthologised in *The Opening of Borders* (World Congress of Poets), *Time's Collision with the Tongue, New World Tattoo, The Nightjar* (Newcastle Poetry Prize) and *Billabong* (Poland).

'Dwelling in the Shape of Things' was separately published as a chapbook in the Vagabond Press Rare Object series.

Grateful thanks for support from the Literature Board of the Australia Council and for a Writer's Fellowship at Varuna, which has enabled me to complete this work.

Many thanks to Julian Merrow-Smith for generous permission to use his painting *Still Life with Irises*.

The poem 'Seven Devils' takes its title from and is loosely based on the Finnish documentary by director Pirjo Honkaslo.

Other books by the same author:
  Abundance (1992)
  Black Night With Windows (1994)
  Dwelling in the Shape of Things (1999)
  Oyster: from Montparnasse to Greenwell Point (2000)

Nicolette Stasko has published three volumes of poetry, winning the Anne Elder Award in 1993 and being short listed for the NSW Premier's Prize and the National Book Awards. Her work is widely anthologised and she has read at many literary events both nationally and overseas. She is also a reviewer, essayist, teacher and the author of the recent best selling non-fiction, *Oyster: from Montparnasse to Greenwell Point*. She lives in Sydney, where she is currently working on her next poetry collection and researching a book on Australian art.

For D and J

CONTENTS

IV

V

The drunk sells his coat.
The thief sells his mother.
Only the poet sells his soul to separate it
from the body that he loves.
            —Tomaž Šalamun *Folk Song*

Throw away the lights, the definitions,
And say what you see in the dark
            —Wallace Stevens *The Man with the Blue Guitar*

I

Ashes

All over the world
poets are going up in flames
leaving
little piles of ashes
in the shape of mountains
it seems we do not notice
their going
so much else is ablaze
but the darkness
is growing and
it is not our eyes
who will be here
to help us see?
to be the mole of the wind
reminding us of death's bright clothes
pointing out
where the stars used to be
from under the glare of so many
busy street lamps

Another Quarrel with the Self
for Alan and Eva

> *...What precisely is it*
> *About the time of day it is, the weather, that causes people to*
> *   note it painstakingly in their diaries*
> *For them to read who shall come after?*
> —John Ashbery *Grand Gallop*

Black   low rumble
argument of a thunderstorm
becoming as it moves towards you
the electric flash
trees distressed as you for once are not
sitting quietly
at a desk before a garden window
remembering the forecast
which called for rain
some things are predictable
though not this inner turbulence silently
contained   already the day encumbered
with strewn garbage and old dogs
buses roaring past
the lightning sparking
while you remain watching calmly enough   beginning
to wonder what the fresh white flowers
in the vase would look like
turned to ash and the green leaves
no longer green what time the train

4

departs tomorrow to return you to that place
where they must now be
experiencing the same fat drops crash
and spread   seeing this same forked flame
the bang on the celestial drum but surely
could not be feeling
this   as again the purple
iris is blown over in the pond
and slowly slowly sinks
while you coolly deliberate
whether to rescue it
or not

After Many Sleepless Nights

I

In dreams ivy grips the stones
stones become dust
death is all around us
your sister's mind
sprouting tumours
like mushrooms
a future we cannot
begin to contemplate even
our own though
the days ahead
seem clear enough
with diaries filled bills paid
a destination that keeps receding
until you climb the final
hill and the sea spreads out
below you
the town distant
shimmering in summer heat

II

the face of the moon rises
a cooling sun

benign above the big pines
the train stops
a passenger gets off

black currawong
among the fallen red
leaves between the black
bodies of the trees
the persimmon blazes
all its golden flames
catching and holding the wind
I am typing out pain
have almost forgotten it now
another
voice is speaking

III

tonight the moon
is winnowed with cloud
it hides its face and spokes its
wheel of light
into the dark sky
we are alone
in this vast space
until the day unloosens
memories of the night before
while we slept
some green creature

(a frog?) braved the cold
desert of dry leaves
and spent grass
to leave a fragile lily of eggs
floating like bubbles
in the small pond
where the fish used to be
and now are gone suffocated
eaten by birds
or grown wings

IV

I have no answers
only regret and ashes
dreams of scratching
thick glass
among the leaves
a window in the earth
hard as onyx
and making no mark
trying to see
down to the depths
never getting beyond
the dull glazed surface
a kookaburra laughs
a small dog barks
every walk here leads to a cliff
red raw teeth collared with green

8

like some great sleeping
animal half-buried
half exposed under the passing
blue
on the opposite side of the world
you struggle
with your own deaths
(only one of us will know the other's)
places I cannot imagine
fill your eyes

V

above the pond
a kookaburra waits staring
down for hours as if
it could will the flash
and movement
of those lost golden scales
while in the neighbour's yard
a mountain of ash
is still smoking
from the pile of burnt cuttings
and branches lopped
on Anzac Day   flames
reflected in the window pane
for a moment I thought the house
was burning
and leapt up

all morning there had been
crackling and small explosions
I did not recognise
in the icy cold
and rain
such fires are enough
to remind you
how terrible the art
of resurrection

A Single Ascension

Valido per una sola corsa in ascensore L.300
                    (biglietto—Città d'Urbino)

There are windows
onto every night
some full of starlight
moonlight   some
empty
if I throw open these shutters
an ancient town below me sleeps
terracotta rooftops glow
like embers
in the last rays of the sun
the air is cold and clean
across on the green hilltop
an apple tree blossoms white
and lovers embrace
oblivious to their dying
bells ring the hours
and in my pocket
a ticket
for the single ascension
to this place where
Raphael walked
on roads that float off
into cloud   all streets meet
beneath the ducal palace   terraces
rooms full of grace and light

of paintings
where cathedral steps
are an alabaster bed
of chambered ammonites
curled like ladies' ears   all
women are beautiful here
with long
Botticellian hair dark eyes
here dark cypresses
seam the sky   as if
there had never been
a rift between
heaven and earth

Death of Blue

1

Eyes open
after four days of fevered sleep
a crown of candles
burns on the dresser
twelve blue iris
incandescent
in the morning light seemed
a sign of something
a gift from the world
unasked for
unmortgaged   now
with wild
abandoned wings they fly
and settle like
bright swallows
around the room
send a message I beg
we are!
we are!
they sing

2

Where does one find
a word
for such a blue
this iris-colour that exists
in dreams
where is the word
for flesh of seraphim
luminous as a child's eyes
would melt
between human fingers
tissue of sky of star
of this earth and not of this earth
O white despair

3

Irises begin to darken
the way eyes do
in certain moods
in certain light
their yellow centres turn
to tarnished gold
they do not lose their petals
as other flowers
but curl back
into themselves
to the place

before they were born
withdrawing
all the blue
from the world

A Moment
for Inez Baranay

Who could forget
the drift of jacaranda blossoms

dropping like blue violet rain
the bright red flower of your mouth!

yet hanging in the wind
like a ticking watch

I decided against flowers
blinded by the glittering sun

certain of the way they fade
so that even the fishermen are leaving

such things are not projections
a person walking past a mirror

turns away or sees another
whose eyes are not their own

but some stranger's looking out at them
struggling to be acknowledged

the way a rebellious vine
rears up into the sky

as a straight-backed chair
is chaste and severe as death

as a single red leaf glows
in the tree at sunset

like a heart

II

On the Economy of Crying

When I cry it is never enough
when you cry it is always too much

we can't listen to anyone else's
crying we don't get paid for

perhaps we could measure tears
in bottles lined up on the windowsill

gauged by the litre glistening in glass
instead of wasted on a face   maybe

the government could put a tax on tears
user pays and all that

we could grow things
with all this crying   pumpkins and

sunflowers which require
a lot of tears   the prediction

for a second deluge is favourable
otherwise   just remember

make them pay up
nothing   is for free

January 18th

after Raymond Carver

Today
I wake up and look out of the window
for some reason I am surprised
to see the sun
I go for a walk which starts out
pleasantly enough
but becomes hot and long
my arm hurts
when I get home I remember
the dog has thrown up
just inside the gate
a glob of whitish yellow stuff
like butter
garnished with green
blades of grass
I need to get rid of it
but first I have to get
a bucket of disinfectant
to soak the nozzle of the hose
on which some prowling tom has shat
(touching I'm told
I could go blind
or develop any number
of fatal diseases)
from there it should be easy
but no

the nozzle is clogged
and no water comes out except
everywhere over me
everywhere but from the place
it should
I fix that
then try again
the bright blue thing
moves like a snake
in the sparse grass and weeds
I start to wash away the spot
the hose kinks and stops
once then twice and
I give up

in between
I go back and forth to my study
and read poetry
some by Zbigniew Herbert
Raymond Carver
and wonder why
life has to be so grim
so serious
(war oppression alcoholism death—
yet   these are my favourite poets
for the moment)
where's the levity
the jokes?
yesterday I saw a psychiatrist
for the second time

and told him about my miserable
birth and infancy
I said my childhood was happy
basically
we discussed anti-depressants
for the good part of the hour
I'm supposed
to see him again
next Tuesday

Long Distance

for Karen

You sit up late
to call
and say you have
a heart condition
I remember when
your first child was born
they told you that
and it has slept
quietly inside you
until now
so you black out
and fall
they've taken away
your big shiny car
and I see you stranded
on that small island
floating in a sea of snow
cold blankness and early dark
unable to help
do anything
but sit at the end
of a telephone line
in this unrelenting heat
and try to make you laugh
at past follies
mine and yours

especially the one
where we thought
we'd live
forever

Stones
for Gay Bilson

When I was a kid
I spent hours gathering
the ugliest least-promising pebbles
smashing them open
with a hammer   the pieces wildly flying
endangering my sight
always looking for the hidden
heart   a secret within
crystal or quartz   veins
running through
like runic maps
now I give my daughter
thunder eggs moss agate silver ore from
the Lucky Friday mine
she goes with me to a friend's house
where smooth brown river stones
are served for lunch
tapped open gently
a lotus leaf unfolds
from among the sandy fragments
blooming quail fish rice
the scent of coriander and lime

Some Windows

Grey stone
window upon window
of the opposite apartment block
in Montparnasse
television screens
a set of frames
that life walks in and out of
strange as the plaster 'David'
on one ledge miraculously
unblemished by rain or pigeons
but changed to an
ill-proportioned gnome
by the simple reduction in size

One day I watched
a dark-haired woman
wearing a pink blouse
with a deep V
I could almost read
the medallion that gleamed
between her breasts
a French Vermeer
bending as she ironed
all day steam rising
and floating from the window
into a white sky

her bright form the only relief
against the grey
except for the slice of melon
in the Greek's shop
on the street below

Once   in another window
a young woman rose
Venus from the rumpled sheets
and stood for a moment
naked with her back to us
unloosed hair cascading
her fleshiness breathtaking
until the curtains closed
we were having lunch
and waited
for the smell of sex to mingle
with *vin ordinaire*
the *chèvre* and bread

Not all was so spectacular
someone painting late at night
an empty flat by lamplight
a student reading
at a desk all day
I wanted to call across to him
life does not last that long
but of course never did

Some windows
in all the time we watched
never showed
a single sign of movement
and might in fact
have lately been
abandoned by the dead
their pure white
blinds drawn down
blank   indescribable
even in
this French *cahier*
in this Paris-bought ink

Fish and Jalepeños

Fat green jalepeños
tinged with gold
hang like lanterns
on the bush

thinking to pick one
it dissolves in my hand
a pearled husk
of liquid decay

falls to the ground
each the same at a touch
an unseen slit
down one sleek side

rotting from the white
seeds and pale flesh
outwards to the skin
what has secretly taken

a bite from each one
like a child
with a chocolate box
what has crawled within

and hidden deep
in the pulpy globes
behind their waxy
translucent walls?

the fish in the pond
are eating the lily leaves
they have swallowed all the weed
and still skim the bottom

sifting the algae or
sucking the surface
their small round mouths
like vacuum cleaners

everything is hungry
as I am hungry
for words for the ripening
red fruit

but all seems dying
empty
spent

Notes of the Pillow

for there is no perfection in life
just as there is no life without death
                    —Sen Shui

In the beneficent tomb
let there be beautiful objects
exquisite bowls of ivory brass or glazed
celadon but empty
of rice and
lotus blossom
elaborately carved screens
through which no light can pass
no eye can see
let there be musical instruments
a whole orchestra
of the most precise
most delicate vessels of sound and wind
clappers removed
one string snapped
a thousand keys intact
and a single
broken

III

The Sea Horse

...whenever a thing changes and alters its nature
at that moment comes the death of what it was before
                    —Lucretius

Everything was the same the house
unchanged   the trees with
the same light flickering
between the leaves
brown green and silver
and yet nothing was the same
we carried some malaise with us
that showed in the sky despite
the tiny sugar glider
with huge liquid eyes
flying to its tree each night
under a pale sickening moon
the sky rinsed of stars

a day
boiling and still
pressure-cooker
of mizzling black specks
furry clinging to eyes and mouth
the fickle wind giving false relief
a liar flaying skin   sand
grinding pupils
beneath closed lids
along the curve of beach

we walked as usual
avoiding the string of bluebottle beads
dull glass sails once windpulled
collapsing into the heat
hair-fine whips straggling down into the sea
as if they would not give up
not even
in that awful death
on the rocks a pair of oyster catchers
sooty black   their orange-red beaks the size and shape
of wooden stakes
dancing around something—
two eels baking
their living flesh drying into leather straps
we could have worn for belts
one tiny and curled worm-like as if torn
from its mother's gut
the large one stiff as a stick
with gaping mouth needle teeth

behind thick gathering clouds
the sun disappears
stillness   like before an eclipse
or earthquake
when all the birds stop singing
and beings hold their breath

a wave washes up
the tattered cloth slowly drags away
leaving a stranded sea dragon

the size of my hand
longer with the spiral tail   luxurious
as a bridal train
a whole jewelled invention
finished in weed-like fins
of topaz and amethyst
brilliant upon the head
comical as tiny arms
protruding
from an organ-grinder's chest
above a swollen belly
iridescent snakeskin stretched
over clearly delicate ribs
a perfect horse face too purely bred
narrow long with nostrils flared
its mouth equine hanging open

we put it in seawater
in a shallow plastic dish
some vague attempt
to save this strange creature thrown by storms
from the ocean depths
lying there while we gazed
its naked eye a cooling ember
staring with neither pathos nor regret
(those human traits)
the mouth closed
a few small bubbles exhaled
the magical beast now at the mercy of flies
colours dimming like lights

we carried it back to the beach dug
a hole in the sand
and covered it with a rock
to keep away the scavenger birds
and mark the place

nothing of him that doth fade
the sea dragon still floats
in my mind
as it had in the blue dish
as it had in the sea
and will not
be buried

On the Phenomenon of Colour

Black the colour
of mourning distinguishes
survivors
from the dead
and in dreams
indicates only
minor misfortune
so violet
is the colour of the soul
according to Dante
who surely saw it
as a shadow before or after him
or as a vague haze
between his eyes
what then is the colour
of sorrow
the sky on these days
neither blue nor grey
but a kind of empty white
merely a backdrop
the blank page   white
the colour
of clothes we once
buried the dead in
the colour of calamity
these too-delicate flowers

on the table   bursting
from their veined leaves
like trumpets   wings
of undiscovered insects
their thin white stamen
so purely white
they are not
to be believed
and soon will be a memory
the shade of separation
the sign of detachment

when will we know red?

Days

for Bruce Beaver

*People who do this are always working. They are not
ashamed to appear idle.*
　　　　　　　—Louis Zukofsky *Poetry*

Day 1

The grace of day wasted
through infirmity
and lack of will
with nothing left
to do but walk
I have no map
the steep path leads down
to an unknown place
a thick marsh bridged over with planks
two boys' shining heads
just visible between the reeds
intently bent on catching
frogs or fish
debris of cockatoos　　the broken seeds
and scoured leaves
under all the big pines and gums
one's black trunk
furred with a fine bright ruff
of green then
the scalded cliffs and thick-treed

43

valleys cradling cloud
I carry the shock of neon-purple berries
like miniature eggplants glowing
in the gloom of the rainforest
a currawong wing
shorn clean off
lying on the ground
as if pointing a direction
through the vast expanse
of deserted golf course
the clipped and cut order an oasis
and yet here I am lost
if this were a dream
I might think there was some
meaning
but I am wide awake
at least the day redeemed

Day 2

Today the forest surrounding us
is veiled in mist
mysterious chiaroscuro
of light and dark
of low lying cloud
filling the spaces
with white
fine rain deepening the green
and brown of trees

to black
and black the shadows of birds
which detach themselves
a pair of wings
just glimpsed
the ominous drone of an earth mover
persists   I have not been alone
for so long
in years

Day 3

The wind continues to tear at the trees
batter the house
then subsides as it has this moment
everything waits   a besieged town
for the next assault
we are tensed holding our breaths
last night our sleep disturbed
by a knocking at all the windows and doors
trying to get in
bringing us dreams of poems
that will never be written
and hover over our poor heads
like soft wings
mothers' voices singing
to their lost youth
the light above our beds
was golden and black

and we could not wake nor grasp it
the spirit shivered
and turned one way
then the other
until all the places were used up
and what was left
was the awful roaring
still trying to get in

Day 4

Last night low clouds drifted
back and forth
the house sailing
among them as if at sea
we sat before a fire
and talked of infinity—
of death   where all that makes us
what we are   goes
yesterday morning
a black cockatoo
sat on a branch outside my window
I could see its red crest
the day grey marked by rain
mist like ghosts moving between
the huge trees
voices   the sound of bird cries
today I woke to find
the sun shining

and I am more alone than I have ever been
death is not the problem
nor nothingness
it is the shadow
existing side by side always
with the light
that the rose is not enough
that the soul is lost to itself   a feeble creek
flowing into brackish weeds

Day 5

These waves, in the sun, remind me of flowers:
The lily's piercing white,
The mottled tiger, best in the corner of a damp place
           —Theodore Roethke *The Long Waters*

Hidden in a back corner of the neglected garden
which makes me want to scrabble
on my knees
between the cement paths
pull weeds and plant herbs renew
what was once flourishing
marjoram oregano sage
dry and flowering
behind some bushes I am startled
by a stand of tiger lilies
ferocious fiery orange
in the bright sunlight seeming like Alice
in Wonderland to rear up at me

47

not with animosity
only equal surprise and curiosity
my scissors itched
and down three stalks came
into my arms
knocking off the black pearls
I thought were snails
huddled in each leaf notch
carried to my room peach gladiolus shy
and delicate as a bride
mingle in the vase
with these wild creatures—
unafraid *flagranté*
their petals curled like a beautiful
young girl's lip
raised spots of a big cat licking itself
the long stamen ending in rust-coloured fury
exclamation point   tongues!
I want to call them
'the young girl's hair'
but there is no softness
the stiff pods unforgiving
I look down at my hands ink—
and now saffron-stained   then see clearly
my glasses on each black pearl
a fecund oval seed

Day 6

Two boats sail silently
across the garden toward the house
the white mist swirls
about them like an ocean
and hangs from purple sails
like rags
in one Odysseus
heading to the island where
he will pour libation for the dead
wine blood-red
into the thirsty sand
the smaller boat is empty
it waits in the shallows
a door blows open
all I must do
is leave my room walk down
the stairs and two stone steps
still warm with sun
take the helm in my hands
and set the slackening sails
to go from this place
under a milky sky
under a moonless night
past the black flags of fishermen
marking their nets
in the midst of a vast
and glittering sea

Day 7

Blessed the blue sky
and reading in bed
the hot cup of tea
blessed the good sleep
undisturbed by dark dreams
waking replenished   the soul
slipping easily into the day
as a body slips
into a clear stream
an aging gently into grace
blessed be the other people in the house
who tread lightly as ghosts
but are corporeal beings
rarely seen
blessed the magnificence
of tiger lilies bristling in the sun
blessed the ability to work
scribbles that will come
into some shape
blessed be the earth mover
not moving on Sunday
cockatoos gone with their screaming
elsewhere
blessed be the time alone
but not forever   blessed
the green blades of grass
and the quiet makers

A Little Shelter
for JS Harry

Everything eventually
finds some resting place
the shabby ibis
with its overcrowded nest
of enormous
ugly darlings jostling
in the cocos palm
rain working its way
into the dry dark core
of trees sighing finally
into intricate veins of leaves
street kids borrowing
for a little while
the small shelter of an overpass
their ragged blankets
hung up in bleak defence against
the glare of lights
and traffic noise
though little use
against mosquitoes breeding
in the slow storm water
which runs below   feeding
freely on thin blood
and so you are moving
toward infinity
the place that has no name

and refuses mapping
there are no directions in the stars
there may be consolation
in the wind

Mudcrabs

I

Mudcrabs are in season it seems
on my birthday here
strange to me still as
no new green on the trees
no breaking fields of lilies
instead
pewter skies and rain
spreading rust spent leaves

I have been bleeding
now for fourteen days
omen of age
a sign of something more?
mudcrabs for the moment
make me forget

as we prepare to
shatter the dull grey
soon turned to red
armour that holds
feathers of the sweetest flesh
hidden within
and fanning out from
outsized claws

that once made
their own kind of death

growing from decay
and oozy mud   feathers
white as roses
you brought me
for my birthday
glowing on my desk
fully opened
their centres crab-coloured
each petal translucent
in the foil light
of morning   when
I had to touch them
to know
if they were real
as mudcrabs scratching
in the crate
huge and heavy as lead
smelling of mangroves
and brute life
as white roses
of sky and death

II

I had forgotten
how sentient they are

how on delicate back legs
they lift eyes claws and whole
iron body in defence
at any approach
how mouths bubble
like a feeding infant's

being used to food that is dead
packaged in plastic and cold
I try not to think of
the scrabbling in the pot
as water boils
refusing to allow them pain
refusing any feeling except
anticipation and greed
Sade my neighbour
even in this

mantle lifts—
a shallow offering bowl
soft grey lungs lined up
like teeth or tusks
a face with once mobile eyes
disintegrates
beneath my fingers
cracking the now bright painted
shell and sucking the flesh
strength and resistance
of carapace!

I had forgotten the fine
rain of juice and sea water
the floor covered
in flying shards wet
as a labour ward
the strong ocean smell

this morning my hands
ache strangely   are bruised
I had forgotten that ancient
savage lust

IV

'Plaza en la Colonia del Sacramento'
after Jorge Damiana

That white building
gleaming in the moonlight
making its complicated shadows
across the plaza   a sky
hung like black velvet curtain
behind it
or the grey dove
quietly absorbing
a small piece of the night
why should I try
to describe it
or even understand
rather   let it enter
remain there forever
or pass through me
clean as a sharp blade
going somewhere else

Dwelling in the Shape of Things

Meditations on Cézanne

I

The blue vase leans
a little
to the left   its ruffled lip revealed
as if a lady's petticoat
it is a blue we love   proving
there is innocence
three tentative apples
trying to keep from sliding
across the slanted tabletop
shyly huddle
closer
to what may be heaven—
a blue-rimmed plate and ink-
bottle clearly secretive
then we realise this is a tilting world
the weight of irises
pulling everything away
from the centre
in spite of the red heart
pinning it like an arrow

II

Here is water

how strangely the bather places
his hands
upon awkward hips
elbows right angles quietly
quartering the canvas
and steps hesitantly from the
solid rocks into
a liquid world of pearl blue and opaline grey as if
he fears some dissolution
this is not a swimmer
but half a land creature
with its thin arms and narrower shoulders
above the powerful legs
of a *bicycliste* used
to controlling his element

III

Seated in a chair which rises like a flower
out of the deeply patterned rug
at once the sea
and a field of waving poppies
a pink and gilt chair no less amazing
than the half turned figure in black its cushioned arms
    embrace

alive with fondness
the eye takes in hands   entwined fingers become
many-limbed animals coupling
and down the angled legs
crossed casually to the slippers one not quite but almost
    dangling
from the relaxed and jaunty foot
those soft old slippers which say everything
we may have missed
the face
but never the red pear shapes
distracting the wallpaper behind it
or the elaborately framed pictures
or the little chest of drawers'
warm brown marquetry

IV

It is the eyes
and the dark mouth enclosed within
a pod of blue   a shadow
always behind
the left shoulder
wherever we walk
we can feel it there
terrible and light
as the mist above a lake in morning
grey of such tenderness
if we could only turn!

the crosses hanging around our necks
would not be so heavy
and so strange
hands which lie
like weapons in our laps

V

The peace of apples

an ivory-handled knife waits patiently
a level horizon   everything
is as it should be
stillness
of clear water in a glass

grapes like an army of children
tumble in a bowl
afraid of nothing
we can hear their shouts and the gentle reprimands
of their teachers
standing quietly by

rounded shapes achingly imperfect
how they all belong to each other!
red as the glow through closed lids
or between fingers held up to the sun
pale spring and yellow green   a soft evening sky
full of the winging of doves

VI

The yellow straw hat sits uneasily
ridiculously
on the head
full lips and sliding eyes
in a fleshy face we recognise
as one of our own
even though the black coat takes up too much space
and we are ashamed
such grossness feeding on the innocent
eating up too many   entirely
certain of its place in the universe
the background recedes   ears burn and eyebrows arch
we must never forget this is
a painting not a portrait however
it seems to be one
a hat assumed only for the sake
of contrast against the grey
but it is a business to make
meaning where there is none

VII

How much like sticks the leafless trees of winter are
it takes
all of the little faith we have
to keep believing they will blossom again
at the coming of the sun

here trees are frozen black and unforgiving
yet lithe as a group of dancers
waiting for the notes to begin
a spangle of ice coating their limbs

from a distance an impassive mountain watches
shadowless green of the grove

VIII

It is a time
the clock with no hands massive and black its white face
has become pure as God
floating above the white shroud
draped like a curtain
in stiff folds
deep shadowed creases
hiding what's underneath
on the table a sea-shell's
red gash
in creamy flesh
gaping mouth
a glassy flower rising with fluted wings
the essence of grey
from which all dreams come
blue-grey waves of the Atlantic in winter
dropping to the floor of light
at the centre   small elliptical hole in the canvas
a shout of yellow shining through from

somewhere
a nowhere which is here
how do we feel before it   gazing
awe-struck and in love?

IX

Beyond the barking of a dog
the face is pure oval
above the massive slab of dress with
its dark satin bands
winnowing upwards
a slight inclination of the head
will give you wistfulness
and the modest
covered buttons

X

Is it possible to represent
our feelings so exactly?
the twisted trunks of trees mimic
furiously writhing couples *volupté*
whose embrace offers nothing
but violence
not even in the pale violet blue of the sky
the vulnerable green of the leaves and grass is
there peace or tenderness

only desire
a leaping dog with bared teeth
the screams of a woman being raped
or giving birth
are the same
we would rather believe
these figures might be dancing
and that the one who bends to wake
the sleeper
does so gently

XI

In L'Estaque   those small
houses with their red roofs
a slide of snow threatening to overwhelm them
and the grey-white cloud
running away
the wind blowing
a road going nowhere and in those houses there seems
no warmth
no smoke issuing from the chimneys
shunning the dark swords of trees which rush down the
slope with the melting snow
it is as if the whole world
has been left to the trees

XII

Is it true that our eyes see what
our hearts have conditioned?
this bald dome
rounded and climbable
as a hillside above shoulders of hunched earth and rock
the tentative mouth sunk in a patch of dark beard
the eyes two windows
unaligned and different as those of an old farmhouse
one clear as a baby
one skulking behind a barbed wire gate
crowned with a pattern
of diamonds and crosses
cruel points in drab grey

XIII

At first you don't notice it
only the vertical line of a tree cutting
the picture in half then white vertebrae
ivory comb of aqueduct
the horizontal vector making the eye move outwards into
    nothing or
inwards to the centre and the mountain
which as if just awakened and still violet with sleep
possesses the valley
we would like to go there
descend the steep hill

from where we stand looking
into the soft green and golden places
to be dissolved in a delicate geometry
all things becoming equal

XIV

The alchemist's dream
to make square
what is round   a wave of white cloth
rises up ready
to engulf the little ship
rudderless
with a cargo of ageing apples
while squat and sturdy jars
casting no shadows are
in turn overpowered by a wooden sky
dark with keyholes glowering
a chaste kitchen table with one shy drawer
humbly balances it all

XV

Red-tiled roofs of houses seem
now like old
friends even the plume of smoke rising from a single
narrow chimney
is fixed

in space and time despite its apparent fragility
as are the mountains across the bay
lightly cloaked
with a pure substanceless sky
the other side
of the world   uninhabited   calmly dreaming
like an animal deep in sleep
the mind builds a bridge over dark blue water
but cannot walk on it
distance remains
we stay forever on the peopled shore
content with the view
through a window

XVI

How little we know about one another
each locked in our own delicate case
surrounded by dark scenery
we contemplate
the apples laid out before us
making deep shadows
on a sail of white cloth
like holes in a field of freshly fallen snow
round reddish gold
we do not understand them
only one woman
with a neck curved and vulnerable as a swan's
holds warm fruit in her hands

leaning toward the centre
giving   or taking away
and what difference between such gestures
in the end?
brooding parallel of trees a storm threatens

that last strange gleaming light the sides of our faces
illuminates
a couple walks away into the coming darkness
uninterested
clouds cloth hem edge repeat their shape

One Return

Needles of the casuarina
are pale green hair

white cockatoos
in the trees

like sheets of paper
clean handkerchiefs

unfolding in the wind
all is silent

except the rumbling
of the train past

two old men on dry grass
basking in the sun

seagulls lost
in a grey parking lot

a half eaten melon—
rind of last night's moon

leaves turn purple
in the falling dusk

the train
rumbles on

everything held together
by an eye

V

Holes

How do you write
about emptiness?
about a sky with no clouds
and no moon
each day with no sun

a hole dug in the earth
is not empty
   perhaps
only when
your finger
goes through the hole
in your old jumper
the foot through the sheet...

where
has what was there
gone?
into the mouths and wings
of moths
into the mouse's nest
disintegrated into dust?
no
not even this is
emptiness

Seven Devils

The women
could do nothing
and they ran away
my father took me North

hurry up Tanushka
hurry up and dress
or the mosquitoes
will surely get you shh
shh Tanushka

his long white beard
floating like a shroud over
the frozen river
Father Vassily
appears to me in dreams
he is Tortu
and there is someone else
I do not know but recognise

splashed in my face
the holy water
he wields like a whip my father uses
on the horses that
pull the sled along the icy tracks

to the stone-cold church
cutting the snow in whispers

still she will not kiss
the sacred icon but
four devils have now
left her

it is dark there
so dark I cannot see except the candles
burning in the darkness
and I am roughly dressed
the mosquitoes
will not get me

whose eyes are coal
the cool Madonna waits
around her head gold glimmers
in the shivering light
she does not answer me
even if
I were to ask

snow-bound tundra
and black pine forests
pointing like spears
into the blue-black sky
they do not know I hear it
from inside   there are
at least

a hundred devils left

and they force my head down
she will not kiss the icon
push my head down
my neck is stiff   the fear
in their faces makes me smile
they close their eyes and
Father Vassily
thunders louder
unable to keep us at bay

cunt and *fuck* I should say
then I would be whipped
but I do not speak
my lips are waxed over
like the seals on the huge books
you press my face into
so I can feel
the words
through my forehead

she will not get dressed
she will not kiss the icon
she will be eaten by mosquitoes
she will be blest and unblest

once a grey-brown pony nuzzled
my hand
through a fence

I ride in the whispering sled
I will not say yes
I will not kneel down

the grain of wood
I stare at moves
like a line of black ants
along the window sill
in spring
what will he do when
I begin to bleed and that will be soon
I will want to howl
at the moon sighing
cool and white
a drowned girl's face
above the milky lake

the sweet stink of my body rising
around me thickly
like incense
snorting from the censer
swung in a boy's hands
nostrils of a horse
in early winter light

around my brown fur cap
clapped closely over my ears
my mother and my sister
pray for Tanushka
from somewhere far away

I will not hear
I will not lie down

the long icicles
dripping from the eaves
like Father Vassily's beard
sharp as teeth will pierce me
I will not weep
the mosquitoes will carry
my blood into heaven

From the Centre
after Francis Webb

Bark shed torn skin
broken jaws filled with rotting teeth
earth-scarred
sinned scurrilous army marches
on its belly
rag tag bald and diseased
the moon covers herself
we close our eyes
or they will burn
dust-filled   lost
glimpses of radiance
the river has vomited up
the knuckle bones
of Osiris
fish float belly-up
scales lifting like lids
overhead
the engines of Lucifer
fly in hordes
spewing death
my language inflates—
better blink/wink
refuse to admit
the banality
of evil
we hand over our prayers

and ears
spinning from the centre
into a concrete void
where even darkness
will be developed
and this is what
we've been redeemed for?

December 31st

for Elizabeth Webby and Uli Krahn

One thing I know:
there are no angels
hovering over
the houses in Glebe
no angel
before this year ends
one waits
sometimes forever
for the sounds
of beating wings
a single dropped
feather
but there is no angel here
to fan these last tired
wind-torn days
only piles of books
we read that nobody else reads
and words
plenty of words
the problem is
to choose the true ones
without an angel's help
not fooled by the noise
of clapping mistaken
for wings

or silence
for the muteness
of stones

Three Days in July

1

I've heard the Greeks have
eight words for wind
today I have seen
at least five kinds of it
and tonight a neighbour's tin roof
shining like silver
under a full moon
at noon we gathered shells
from a lion's pelt laid out along the sea
the first one unique
miraculous
then found they studded the beach
like nuggets in a seeded mine
each one perfect   unbelievable
as the first
and now while we read
Selected Letters and *Writers on Art*
our daughter has lain quietly by the fire
for two hours
picking grains of sand
from each delicate
cornet

2

All your life
I have been writing
about you
and will be
for what remains of mine
this morning making us coffee
grinding the beans
with strength
you did not have a year ago
tall and strong
your slim child's body
amazing in its unassuming grace
your face holds no shadows
yet no shadow at your back
instead a small white owl
sits lightly
on your breast
I could wish for you
only one eye to see
what is beautiful and good
but that would be a lie
or rather keep you
as you are now
standing in the shimmering light
under the ancient
spotted gums
throwing stones
at a propped-up board

savouring
the loud astounding
thwack

     3

This last day
I sit flattering the sea
digging holes miles deep
with a stick
in the golden sand
talking myself out
of ambition
desire   allowing the sun
to enter my eyes
and flow out
through my fingertips
the shadow of the forest
at my back   advancing
towards me
like an enemy

The Reef Heron

It is necessary to crouch behind the salt bush so they won't see or hear you and wait until they have gone. It is cool and safe in the shadow. I wrap my black flapping clothes almost all I own about me closer and huddle deeper trying to disappear. For my whole life it has been like this. Darting out into the light and open to get food. My father will not beat me if I stay small. Still I must clean the fish he brings each day dragging the boat up onto the mud. Even when he is on top of me at night grunting and groaning his hot sour breath on my face I can feel my sharp elegant beak making a clean space in the dark. Around my long narrow eye the yellow marking is an arrow and my body thin and perfect smooth pearly grey like smoke so quick he cannot really catch or hold me. I know I have always lived on a clear sweep of beach—white sand and blue sky, the sea sparking right up to the velvet dunes where I build my nest and rest from catching small beetles and crabs, my beautiful long neck stretched out like a dart. Even when I am in the damp house that humps by the bay. Even when I am cold I know that I am meant to go back to tell the angels how hard it is to be human, to live on the earth in the flesh of a body with two arms and legs. To keep your wings hidden and never fly except in your mind sometimes over the water.

The Sound

Emerging from an Abyss, and re-entering it—
that is Life, is it not, Dear?
　　　　　　—Emily Dickinson *letter to Susan*

Out beyond the house
the sound whispers
beyond the tall pine trees
the soft carpet of red needles
a bridge of weathered planks
gilded by the sun is flung
across a delta of black mud and
rivulets fierce from yesterday's rain
the sound of rushing water
under clumps of yellow reeds
thick and matted down
a covey of quail flying up
alarmed
at our passing
to step off into the mud
is to be lost
up to your hips
devoured by mosquitoes
we follow it
to the hard-packed white sand
fine as talcum
rubbed like silk with our walking

and marked by waves
in delicate golden lines
we cannot read
our skin is golden
our hair is on fire in the dying light
the valves of the ocean open and close
like a heart
around the giant hands of oysters
brittle fingers pointing skyward
a graveyard of bones
bleached by the sun
where each year gatherers drown
in the swiftness of the tide
which washes this place clean
and leaves its strange gifts—
driftwood
nestling sea lice
like a lapful of pearls
the cracked bowl of a horseshoe crab
thick-shelled clams
ridged as an old man's fingernail Atlantic-
coloured sand-coloured violet blue
Dafuskie Beaufort Bluffton
this should be home
but it is not
the rare brown pelicans make an arc of air
toward the long arm of sand
the last visible before the sea closes over
and there is only the sea
smooth glassy fields

milky   white
and then molten
a tarnished silver
of old tea sets and mirrors
in damp houses on the mainland
the dark comes down
I could walk out into the sea
and feel the waves wash over my head
there is no choice but to go
back to the house
where my father sits deafly
reading the newspaper
in the zinc light of the TV screen
my mother packing up the plastic
Christmas tree
a corpse to be gotten rid of
such a mess she says
such a mess
it is not yet
even the first
of January

After Wangaratta and Donatello
for Peter Rose

Encumbered sun
it is morning still
the day drenched in blossom
ethereal   white
clouds of golden bees
a Mozart concerto
accompanies the hum
all morning
lolling in bed
the tea not yet cooled
I am reading poems
by a friend
a single red petal from
the hawthorn branch placed
in a vase yesterday
has fallen
on a photograph
like confetti   a bright drop of blood
making what suddenly seems
a Chinese vignette
late spill of cherry trees while
the day stretches endlessly on
your poems have left me
melancholy   joyous
saddened
as the white blossoms drift

slowly one by one
to the dark
indifferent ground

The Kingdom of Sparrows

Two women
in floral house dresses
lean
gossiping
their white shoes
like bright cut paper
fluorescent in the
electric light
of a coming storm

in the kingdom of sparrows
twittering hordes
small as hummingbirds
forage for leftovers
in rubbish bins
peck insects
from weeds along the foreshore

a tiny Japanese man
sits on a collapsible canvas stool
under the massive ficus trees
picking and sorting
the tenderest
dandelion leaves
in the kingdom of sparrows
world without end